RURAL INFRASTRUCTURE SCHEME (RIS) THROUGH VILLAGE PANCHYATS.

SUDHATHANIGAIVEL

XpressPublishing
An imprint of Notion Press

XpressPublishing
An imprint of Notion Press

Old No. 38, New No. 6
McNichols Road, Chetpet
Chennai - 600 031

First Published by Notion Press 2020
Copyright © Sudhathanigaivel 2020
All Rights Reserved.

ISBN 978-1-64869-863-7

I DEDICATE THIS BOOK TO MY BELOVED PARENTS

R.V.KUMARAVELU (Rtd.Thashildar) and K.BUVANESWARI(Home maker),

My Husband S.THANIGAIVEL.(AGRICULTURIST)

Contents

Part 1

Foreword

I hope this book is useful for researchers those who are intrested in Village Panchyat schems and Plans. Moreover this useful to know about the benifits of Local Government in
village level.

Preface

Hai readers,

Rural development aims at finding ways to improve rural lives with participation of rural people themselves, so as to meet the required needs of rural communities. Panchayat is a democratic self-ruled institution of a village, which Gandhiji rightly called the base of the real democracy or village swaraj. Gandhiji's main aim was to open the door of the filings of swaraj even for the last one of under-privileged and deprived persons of the society, which can be possible only through the Panchayati Raj Institutions (PRIs).

Acknowledgements

I Thank to the following Authors who support to publish this book.

BIBLIOGRAPHY

Arvind Kumar Pande, 1994 "Flow of Funds in Panchayat Bankala During the Seventh Five Year Plan", Journal of Rural Development Vol. 13(2), pp. 269 – 278.

B. S. Bhargava, (1979), A Study of Grass Root Leadership in Panchayat Raj Institutions, New Delhi; Ashish, p.88.

B.S. Khanna, (1994), Panchayati Raj in India: Rural Local self Government – National perspective and State Studies, New Delhi: Deep and Deep publications.

Bandhyopadhyay D. (2003), Issues for Twelth Finance Commission, EPW. June 7-13, Vol XXXVIII No.23.

Bharati Pratima Achrya and Remesh Chandra Pande (2002), 'Panchayati Raj Institution in Tamil Nadu', Journals of Rural Development, Vol 21, No 11.

CHAPTER ONE

PANCHYAT RAJ

Abstract

The term Panchyat Raj is relatively new, having originated during the British administration .Raj literally means governance or government. Mahatma Gandhi advocated Panchyat Raj, a decentralized form of Government where each village is responsible for its own affairs, as the foundation of India's political system. His term for such a vision was Gram Swaraj or Village self -goverance. It was adopted by state governments during the 1950s and 60s laws were passed to established Panchyats in various states.

The bridge the exisiting gap in the physical infra- structure in rural areas ,which is critical for sustainable economic development, the Government plans to implement the Rural Infrastructure Scheme (RIS) with the aim of taking up of more roads for better rural connectivity and to stabilize the assets created under MGNRGS. Quality roads and better connectivity are important for maintain the growth momentum. At present under the Mahatma Gandhi National Rural Employment Guarantee Scheme, such works like desilting of ponds, channels, ooranies and formation of roads arinvolvement of contractors and machineries.

CHAPTER TWO

Introduction

Since the Mahatma Gandhi National Rural Employment Guarantee Scheme (MGNREGS) has been extended to all the districts of Tamil Nadu from 1.4.2008 onwards, the Central Government has discontinued the Sampoorna Grameen Rozgar Yojana (SGRY). At present under the Mahatma Gandhi National Rural Employment Guarantee Scheme, such works like desilting of ponds, channels, ooranies and formation of roads are undertaken in Tamil Nadu which are directly entrusted to the people without the involvement of contractors and machineries. In the current scenario, consequent upon the discontinuance of SGRY and implementation of MGNREGS, rural infrastructure works involving intensive material u sage and varied utilization of machinery are not adequately taken up under the existing Centrally Sponsored Schemes. There is a need to stabilize the assets created under MGNREGS. Further, there is a continuous pressing need to undertake structural repairs of Minor Irrigation (MI) Tanks vested with the Panchayat Unions.

CHAPTER THREE

Government Schemes

RIS

'Rural Infrastructure Scheme' (RIS) serves the dual purpose of creating Infrastructure facilities in the village as well as stabilizing the assets created through MGNREGS. It is implemented in all the 3 tiers of Rural Local Bodies (i.e) District Panchayat, Panchayat Unions and Village Panchayats.

DRDA

The District Rural Development Agency (DRDA) has traditionally been the principal organ at the District level to oversee the implementation of different anti-poverty programmes. It is an effective agency at the district level to coordinate and monitor all the Centrally and State Sponsored Schemes implementation. DRDA is a society register under Societies Registration Act. The District Collector is the Chairman

of the District Rural Development Agency. DRDA will be headed by a Project Director who should be in the rank of an Additional Collector or Joint Director of Rural Development. He would be in overall charge of the activities of the DRDA and responsible for interaction with District / State Administration as well as with the Govt. of

India.

The following schemes are being implemented by the DRDA brought out by

The Central Government Schemes

Mahatma Gandhi National Rural Employment Guarantee Scheme (MGNREGS)

Indira Awaaz Yojana (IAY)

Member of Parliament Local Area Development Scheme (MPLADS)

Pradhan Mantri Gram Sadak Yojana (PMGSY)

The State Government Schemes

Namakku Naame Thittam (NNT)

Member of Legislative Assembly Constituency Development Scheme (MLACDS)

Rural Infra Structure (RIS)

Rural Building Maintenance and Renovation Scheme (RBMRS)

Total Sanitation Campaign (TSC)

Scheme Component of Pooled Assigned Revenue (SCPAR)

CHAPTER FOUR

AWARDS

All the habitations that eliminate the practice of open defecation and adopt improved personal hygiene behavior, effective waste management and water conservation will be awarded with cash incentive for population based and incentive will go to village development fund.

Sl.No	details of village panchayats	Incentive Rs. in Lakhs
1	Below 1000	0.50
2	1000 - 1999	1.00
3	2000 - 4999	2.00
4	5000 - 9999	4.00
5	Above 10000	5.00

In the NGP amount should be used for water and sanitation improvement works.

In the NGP amount should be used for water and sanitation improvement works.

NGP Awarded Panchayat Details

Sl.No	Awarded Year	No.of Panchayat Awarded
1	2005 - 2006	1
2	2006 - 2007	6
3	2007 - 2008	41
4	2008 - 2009	8
	Total	85

CHAPTER FIVE

Development Schemes.

The main object of Rural Development Department is to provide Basic Amenities to Rural people and to implement various Development schemes like road works. Drinking Water , street Lights , Construction of School Buildings etc. it plays an Important role in the up liftment of rural unemployed people especially Below Poverty Line and SC/ST people , by providing Integrated Rural Development Programme Loans , TAHDCO Loans , Self Sufficiency Schemes . Also many Women welfare Schemes and Children Welfare Schemes like DWCRA, Moovalur Ramamirtham Ammaiyar Ninaivu Thirumana Udavi Thittam , Iru pen Kuzhandaigal Thittam, and Anjugam Ammaiyar Kalappu Thirumana Udavi Thittam, are implemented by This Departmenr , Also it motivates savings among rural people by conducting R.D. Camps and pay Roll Savings Schemes.

Public Services provided by the Office/Department
Social Education
Construction & Maintenance of Panchayat Union School Buildings.
Maintenance of Panchayat Union roads.
Planning permissions
Issuing Licence to Dangerous and offensive Trades.

Small Savings Scheme

Moovalur Ramamirtham Ammiyar Ninaivu Thirumana Udavi Thittam

Thamizhaga Arasin Anjugam Ammiyar Kalapu Thirumana Udaiv Thittam.

Thamizhaga Arasin Iru pen kuzhandigal pathukappu Thittam

Thanizhga Arasin Ezhai Viddhavai Magal Thirumana Udavi Thittam

Eye Camp

Implementing Bio gas Scheme .

Fixing of Chulha and promoting non conventional energy sources.

TIDCO Schemes

Providing one light to one hut.

Providing Scholarship to SC/ST women Students in Schools

Self Employment Scheme for SC/ST.

Inspection of Co- operative Societies and creation of New Co-operative Societies

Maintenance of Animal Husbandry

Flood Relief Schemes

Drought Relief Schemes

Conducting Panchayat Election .

Providing Drinking Water Facilities

Puratchi Thalaivar MGR Noon Meals Scheme

Basic Amenities provided by Village Panchayats such as

Road works , Drinking water , Sanitation Programmes. Collection of House Tax, Street Lights are maintained by panchayat Unions. State Finance Commission Grant Works. Jawahar Velai Vaippu Thittam 15% Anna Marumalarchi Thittam.

MLA Local Area Development Programme, MP Local Area Development Program

Namakku Name Tittam

Employment Assurance Schemes .

Central Rural Sanitation Program.

10th Finance Commission Scheme

Implementing works recommended by District Panchayat

Jawahar Velai Vaippu Thittam 70% works

Entegrated Rural Development Program.

Development of women and Children in Rural areas.

Indira Awas Yojana.

Providing water supply and drainage Street Light Maintenance though the Panchayat Providing Comprise water supply works formation .and Maintenance of Roads Contraction of School and panchayat Buildings and Bridges, Strengthening of M-I-Tanks , Constriction of Group House to in weaker (All Communities) and Contraction of Govt. aids to in Poor Familiars under Moovalar Ramamirtham Ammaiyar Tirumana Udavithittam. Improvement of Panchayat management and Department of Works - Link Roads, Bridges, Buildings, Water Supply. Women and children development.

CHAPTER SIX

Other Services

1. Permission for Repairs of House/Structure
2. License for Hotels/ Shops/ Restaurant/ Eating House/ Coffee House/ Sweet Meat Shop/ Bakery/ Boarding etc.
3. Permission for construction of factories/ Installation of Machinery.
4. License for using any place for Trade, Business or Industry.
5. License for places for disposal of Dead Bodies:
6. Licensing of Shops

Certificates issued by the Village Panchayat

1) Income Certificate
2) Birth / Death Certificate
3) Occupancy Certificate
4) No Dues Certificate
5) Non-Availability of Birth or Death Certificate
6) Residence Certificate
7) Character Certificate
8) Dependency Certificate
9) Poverty Certificate
10) Divergence Certificate

11) Bonafide Fisherman Certificate
12) Occupation Certificate

Other Services

Grant of Licence for Construction/ Reconstruction of any structure:

Any person intending to erect,reconstruct,alter or modify any structure shall make an written application to the panchayat in accordance with the following order issued by the Government in this regard.

In order to simplify the procedure for the grant of permission for the construction of building, the government is pleased to issue the following instruction for strict compliance of the panchayat or the concerned authority.

1) Every person seeking permissiom for construction of the building shall prepare four sets of building plans and drawing and submit the same to the panchayat along with all necessary documents as required by the Goa Daman & Diu Village Panchayat, {Regulation of Building} Rules, 1971.

2) The Village Panchayat Secretary or any other person authorized by Panchayat in this behalf shall acknowledge the application. The Panchayat Secretary shall scrutinize the application and place the same before the Sarpanch. Within 2 days from the date of receipt of the application. In case if the application is complete in all respects, the Sarpanch shall forward the plains and drawing to the Town Planner of the concerned taluka in duplicate and simultaneously one set of plans & drawing drawing to the Assistant Engineer of PWD/Technical officer. In case the application is incomplete. The Panchayat Secretary shall return the same to the applicant within the week with the

direction to resubmit the application after complying with the observation rased by the panchayat.

3) The Town Planner and the Technical Officer shall communicate their comments/views within two weeks from the date of the receipt of the plans and drawing from the panchayat.

4) The Town Planner shall scrutinize the plans and convey his comments on the following aspects:-

a} The area of the plot

b} The area allowed to be converted by the Dy. Collector

c} The permissible FAR

d} FAR proposed for construction

e} Height of the building.

f} Number of units allowed and their purpose.

g} Total built up area.

h} The area kept for car parking, open space etc.

i} Set back approved North, South, East, & West.

j} Area of the existing structure incase of reconstruction.

k} Access to the proposed construction

l} Whether any traditional access or footpath are existing

m} The zone in which the proposed construction falls and any other information which may be relevant

Permission for Repairs of House/Structure:

i) A panchayat may grant permission for the repairs of a house/structure without the approval of Town & Country Planning Department within the existing plinth area. However the Panchayat should satisfy itself that the applicant is the owner of the house and has furnished all the other required documents before grant of such permission.

ii) In order to keep an effective control and avoid any misuse of such repairs license granted by the Panchayat,

formats for granting such a license, Inspection Report and the Application form for issue of repairs permission have been prescribed by this Department vide Circular No.15/77/DP/CIR/200/6983 dated 6.9.2002.

iii) The Panchayat shall ensure that the repairs permission is issued only to the existing houses which were constructed after obtaining valid licenses or the house is recorded in the House Tax Register for the last more than five years. iv) The Panchayat shall compulsorily obtain and retain in the file of the concerned party, the details of repairs, the Inspection Report and the copy of the permission granted in the prescribed formats.

License for Hotels/ Shops/ Restaurant/ Eating House/ Coffee House/ Sweet Meat Shop/ Bakery/ Boarding etc:

A renewable license for hotels/shops/restaurants/ eating house/ Coffee house/ sweet meat shop/ bakery/ boarding, etc. is issued by the Panchayat under section 70 of The Goa Panchayat Raj Act,1994. A person requiring such a license should apply to the Sarpanch. After carrying out necessary inquiry, the matter is placed before the Panchayat body which through its resolution decides on the issue of such permission. The Secretary shall thereafter implement the resolution of the Panchayat.

Permission for construction of factories/ Installation of Machinery:

A renewable permission for construction or establishment of any factory, workshop or workplace or for installation of machinery or manufacturing plant is issued by the Panchayat under section 68 of The Goa Panchayat Raj Act, 1994. A person requiring such permission should apply to the Sarpanch. After carrying out necessary inquiry, and after verifying all the relevant documents, the matter is placed before the Panchayat Body which through its resolution decides on the issue of such permission. The Secretary shall thereafter implement the resolution of the Panchayat.

License for using any place for Trade, Business or Industry:

A renewable license for construction or establishment of any factory, workshop or workplace or for installation of machinery or manufacturing plant is issued by the Panchayat under section 69 of The Goa Panchayat Raj Act, 1994. A person requiring such a License should apply to the Sarpanch. After carrying out necessary inquiry, and after verifying all the relevant documents, the matter is placed before the Panchayat Body which through its resolution decides on the issue of such license The Secretary shall thereafter implement the resolution of the Panchayat.

License for places for disposal of Dead Bodies:

A renewable license for disposal of dead bodies is issued by the Panchayat under section 95 of the Goa Panchayat Raj Act, 1994. A person or community or organization requiring such a license should apply to the Sarpanch. The application in such a case should indicate all details such as the plan showing the locality, boundary and extent of the area, the name of the owner, locality or person interested, the system of management and other details as may be called for by the Panchayat. After carrying out necessary inquiry and after verifying all the relevant documents, the matter is placed before the Panchayat Body which through its resolution decides on the issue of such license. The Secretary shall thereafter implement the resolution of the Panchayat. Registration of such burial or burning grounds is also required to be done under section 94 of The Goa

Panchayat Raj Act, 1994.

Licensing of Shops:

A renewable license is issued by the Panchayat for permanent and temporary shops under section 71 of The Goa Panchayat Raj Act, 1994. Any person requiring such a license should apply to the Sarpanch. After carrying out necessary inquiry, and after verifying all the ownership documents, the matter is placed before the Panchayat body which through its resolution decides on the issue of such permission. The Secretary shall thereafter implement the resolution of the Panchayat.

.

No Objection Certificates (NOCs) issued by the Village Panchayat:

Any person desirous of obtaining the following NOCs may apply to the concerned Village Panchayat. The required NOCs are issued by the Panchayat after taking into consideration objections, if any, from the villagers and verifying the ownership/title documents in respect of the property.

All NOCs issued are duly registered in the Register maintained for the purpose and are issued only after passing of are solution to that effect by the Panchayat.

1)NOC for Water Connection

2) NOC for Electricity Connection

3) NOC for House Repair

4) NOC for Road Cutting

5) NOC for running General Stores

6) NOC for running Bar/ Liquor shop

7) NOC for Establishment

Conclusion & Recommendations.

On the basis of statistical analysis of five years data
and practical experience, discussion with various persons
in the field concluded the following recommendations to
be adopted for overcoming problems faced by village
panchayat for its economical strengthening on their own
sources of Income

1)To have mapping of villages along with marking
land levels & maintains Permanent record of works done in
it.

After taking levels to have plan for 100 years underground
drainage system of village which will carry all drain water
& material without problem in pressure & in slope levels of
land. It will help to widen the road on it.

As space of old open drainage system will available
additionally for roads.

This is to be done in complete villages with central & state
funds.

It will help to reduce recurring expenditure   years
together indirectly saving in the funds. Like as above 2nd
life bearing 100 years pipe-line system with same quality &
durability with central& state funds.

Construction of Roads having life of at least 100 years from
central or state funding which will help to avoid yearly
recurring expenditure.

To have use of solar system for streetlights & Gram
Panchayat office from central / state funds, which will
reduce recurring expenditure.

Proper levels of land will help to have proper slope of
drainage system &underground system.

It will avoid health problems arising due to drain, Hygienic
atmosphere will be created in village & reduce in individual
expenditure on health of villagers.

To provide purified water in water supply scheme itself to

villagers with regular & assured sources of water.

Which also helps to villagers to save their time for water collection & also pure water will help to hygienic life & save money on health expenditure.

100% correct property & other tax assessment & its 100% recovery within financial year without fail.

It requires to have public awareness & paying taxation should be fundamental duty of villagers, citizens.

No benefit of any scheme, voting powers, allowed to tax failure.

To see whether grants from upper level are receiving as eligibility of Gram Panchayat or not.

If not demand accordingly with persuasion get it released.

To have charging of various taxes which Gram Panchayat can charge.

To see regular & full recovery of market fees.

To have important places used for shopping / commercial complex- let it on hire that rent should be appropriately increasing trend of market it should be assessed by frequent period of time which will help for assured regular and proper income to Village Panchayat.

To have tree plantation on vacant land which are not used for building purpose or any other roadside also which help to maintain village atmosphere pollution free.

Village roadside should give for raising for grazing grass as a fodder on Auction.

Fixed rates or uniform parameter, which will give money to Panchayat.

Village tanks must transfer to Village Panchayats & these should have auction of tank yearly for fishery on commercial bidding or fixation commercial rates per H.a., which can be good source of income.

Village Panchayat should get some portion; of Road tax

collected by RTO department on same criteria like averagely transport of passengers in tax paid vehicles or some such reasonable criteria.

For implementation of scheme of central & state government at village level some % as agency charges should get to village panchayat in order to meet out its work, expenditure on salary, & contingency at office.

In this way Village Panchayat can become fully economically sound (strength) in two ways. One creating strong long term, durable, qualitative planned infrastructure work with central and state assistance & reduce regular years together recurring expenditure on these items by Village Panchayat like Road, Gutters,water supply & street lights etc.

CHAPTER SEVEN

On the basis of statistical analysis of five years data and practical experience, discussion with various persons in the field concluded the following recommendations to be adopted for overcoming problems faced by village panchayat for its economical strengthening on their own sources of Income

To have mapping of villages along with marking land levels & maintains Permanent record of works done in it.

After taking levels to have plan for 100 years underground drainage system of village which will carry all drain water & material without problem in pressure & in slope levels of land. It will help to widen the road on it.

As space of old open drainage system will available additionally for roads.

This is to be done in complete villages with central & state funds.

It will help to reduce recurring expenditure years together indirectly saving in the funds. Like as above 2nd life bearing 100 years pipe-line system with same quality & durability with central& state funds.

Construction of Roads having life of at least 100 years from central or state funding which will help to avoid yearly recurring expenditure.

To have use of solar system for streetlights & Gram Panchayat office from central / state funds, which will reduce recurring expenditure.

Proper levels of land will help to have proper slope of drainage system &underground system.

It will avoid health problems arising due to drain, Hygienic atmosphere will be created in village & reduce in individual expenditure on health of villagers.

To provide purified water in water supply scheme itself to villagers with regular & assured sources of water.

Which also helps to villagers to save their time for water collection & also pure water will help to hygienic life & save money on health expenditure.

100% correct property & other tax assessment & its 100% recovery within financial year without fail.

It requires to have public awareness & paying taxation should be fundamental duty of villagers, citizens.

No benefit of any scheme, voting powers, allowed to tax failure.

To see whether grants from upper level are receiving as eligibility of Gram Panchayat or not.

If not demand accordingly with persuasion get it released.

To have charging of various taxes which Gram Panchayat can charge.

To see regular & full recovery of market fees.

To have important places used for shopping / commercial complex- let it on hire that rent should be appropriately increasing trend of market it should be assessed by frequent period of time which will help for assured regular and proper income to Village Panchayat.

To have tree plantation on vacant land which are not used for building purpose or any other roadside also which help to maintain village atmosphere pollution free.

Village roadside should give for raising for grazing grass as a fodder on Auction.

Fixed rates or uniform parameter, which will give money to

Panchayat.

Village tanks must transfer to Village Panchayats & these should have auction of tank yearly for fishery on commercial bidding or fixation commercial rates per H.a., which can be good source of income.

Village Panchayat should get some portion; of Road tax collected by RTO department on same criteria like averagely transport of passengers in tax paid vehicles or some such reasonable criteria.

For implementation of scheme of central & state government at village level some % as agency charges should get to village panchayat in order to meet out its work, expenditure on salary, & contingency at office.

In this way Village Panchayat can become fully economically sound (strength) in two ways. One creating strong long term, durable, qualitative planned infrastructure work with central and state assistance & reduce regular years together recurring expenditure on these items by Village Panchayat like Road, Gutters,water supply & street lights etc.

CHAPTER EIGHT

CHAPTER NINE